PRODUCTIVI

BOOK DESCRIPTION

Many people are very busy, but they still find that they are not getting much done. This is because of their mistaken focus on activity rather than productivity; and performance rather than results. When this becomes persistent, frustrations start cropping in.

This book is about productivity – the 'miracle' that make one person's two hours of work worth more than another person's full day's work. It is a miracle if you do not learn. However, if you learn the simple habits of highly effective people, put them into your routine and practice them religiously, you will start living rather than believing the miracle.

The book starts by providing you with information about bad habits that make people less productive. It is only by knowing and understanding this disease (bad habits), its causes, and its symptoms that we can have appropriate cure. In this book, you will learn how to counter bad habits that could be making you less productive and unhappier.

Nothing succeeds without a plan. In this book, you will learn simple plans that you can make to achieve your productivity goals. Planning and setting goals are important to organizing your life, harnessing the power within you, optimizing your productivity and enjoying a balanced stress-free life.

Get this book to learn more about how to optimize your productivity.

GIFT INCLUDED

If you are an entrepreneur, an aspiring entrepreneur, someone who is trying to create additional income stream or even someone who just loves self-improvement books; then you need to read my recommendations for top 10 business books ever. These books read by me have changed my life for the better.

Top 10 Business Books

ABOUT THE AUTHOR

George Pain is an entrepreneur, author and business consultant. He specializes in setting up online businesses from scratch, investment income strategies and global mobility solutions. He has successfully built several businesses from the ground up and is excited to share his knowledge with you. Here is a list of his books.

Books of George Pain

DISCLAIMER

CONTENTS

INTRODUCTION

Productivity is the greatest secret to a rich, healthy and balanced lifestyle. Yet, it is one of those concepts that people mistake the most. If you do not master the art and science of productivity, you will labor like a donkey only to lead a unhappy life like a beast of burden.

This book will show you how to organize your life, harness the power within you, optimize your productivity and enjoy a balanced stress-free life.

This book will enable you to take control of your life and maximize your wealth through productivity.

Keep reading!

BAD HABITS THAT KILL OUR PRODUCTIVITY

Bad habits have been known to lower one's productivity, weakens one's power to achieve optimality and eventually result in an unhappy life. Bad habits are the unwanted garbage that you must scoop off from your environment, both in and out, so that you can enjoy a clean, satisfying, and fulfilling life.

There are many ways to overcome these bad habits and thus ensure that they do not creep in again. These include substitution, sublimation, positive affirmations, and neuro-linguistic programming, among others.

These bad habits can be categorized into:

1. Bad morning habits

2. Bad working habits

3. Bad wake up habits

4. Bad internet habits

5. Bad social habits

6. Bad leisure habits

7. Bad sleeping habits

8. Bad health habits

9. Bad money habits

10. Bad leadership habits

Bad wake up habits

Starting a new day begins with waking up. How you wake up could determine how your day goes. A good day is a setup by good wake-up habits.

The following are some of the bad wake-up habits:

1. Hitting the snooze button

Hitting the snooze button is one of the most common bad wake-up habits. Most people set alarm some 30 minutes to one hour prior to their wake-up time. This way, they consider it ideal in the sense that they will snooze it and have light sleep as they head towards wake-up time. However, this fragments the sleep.

Fragmented sleep leads to sleepiness-related daytime impairment. This lowers productivity during the day.

Solution

The solution is simple – get to bed early enough and set alarm at the latest time you expect to wake up. Do not snooze; get off the bed immediately the alarm rings. The more you practice this the more it becomes habitual. Eventually, your body will be accustomed to it and it will resist any attempt to stay in bed a minute longer after the alarm.

Tuning yourself to wake up immediately after the alarm rings also help to set up your biological clock. You will end up waking naturally without any prompt from the alarm. This is the best thing that can happen to you.

Bad morning habits

Morning is the most important time of the day. It is what you do in the morning that sets up your day. Having bad morning habits will negatively effect your whole day thus lowering your productivity.

The following are some of the bad morning habits:

- Going online to social media immediately after waking up
- Playing video games
- Watching morning news

Bad working habits

It is at work that your productivity should be clearly visible. However, even at work, there are certain habits that contribute to lowered productivity. Unsurprisingly, this is where most bad habits that negatively affect productivity are.

Some of these bad habits include:

1. Multitasking

Multitasking is about doing more than one task at a time. In multitasking, your attention, energy, and effort are shared among the different tasks you are carrying out. More energy and effort are wasted in switching attention from one task to another. Also, more resources are likely going to be wasted (for example, higher risks of accident and damage). You spend more energy in multitasking than you would spend on one task at a time, which leads to mental exhaustion and burnout. All these contribute to lowered productivity and suboptimal outcome.

How to stop multitasking:

- Always endeavor to complete one task at a time
- Stack similar tasks together
- Automate routine tasks

2. Engaging big-picture thoughts during working hours

Big-picture thinking refers to focusing your thoughts on your vision while carrying out tasks. While big-picture thinking is good, it should be done at the right time – before or after work. Big-picture thinking deviates your attention, focus and mental energy away from the task at hand thus resulting in sub-optimality and lowered productivity. Deal with the task beforehand.

How to stop big-picture thinking:

- Focus on the pixels – Focus on elements of your task at hand
- Focus on achieved progress – Instead of looking at the future, look at how far you have come in carrying out the task. This will not only motivate you but also allow you a chance to make quick evaluation and take necessary corrective measures to optimize productivity.
- Consign big-picture thinking to non-working hours – Shut your mind away off the big-picture while working.

3. Not having a work routine

Work routine helps your brain map your work and automate it. Thus, you will spend less mental energy on work with routine than on that which has no routine.

How to overcome it:

- Start working at the same time everyday
- Work from the same place everyday
- Prepare a work schedule and follow it religiously

4. Keeping off the most important tasks until later in the day

Most people avoid dealing with the most important tasks in the morning. This is because most of the important tasks are not appealing. They are scared of the tasks due to how taxing they are to the mind. To the mind, they appear ugly – a 'frog'. This is why these important yet difficult or unappealing tasks are called 'frogs'. Obviously, most people would not like to eat frogs, especially in the morning. Yet, avoiding eating frogs in the morning makes it even tougher to eat them afterward. In the morning, there is sufficient power in the gnashing jaws to crush them.

Eating frogs in the afternoons will most likely be too late, and if not, you are more likely not to finish eating.

Solution

The best remedy is to identify these frogs and isolate them to be your next meal after your morning exercise. At that time, you have sufficient energy from your breakfast, strong muscles from your exercise and the alertness.

5. Being perfectionist

It is natural for everyone to expect a perfect outcome. Yet, such is an ideal that hardly comes to reality. Thus, struggling for perfection is like striving to reach a shinning pool of a mirage ahead of you in order to quench your thirst. You have to learn that a river is never pure; yet, your thirst will be quenched by water from it – not the mirage.

This too applies to your job. Do what meets expectations.

Characteristics of perfectionism:

- Unrealistically high work standards
- Getting off-balance when a standard is not met

How to overcome perfectionism:

- Focus on finishing, not perfecting
- Accept failure when things don't work out

6. Overloading yourself with information

Information overload is a modern-day challenge. Tons of information released on the internet every day. As we become reliant on the internet for information, we are inevitably bombarded by this overwhelming information.

Characteristics of information overload:

- Mental fatigue
- Loss of focus

How to overcome information overload:

- Unplug yourself from sources of overwhelming information
- Pick the best source of information and work on it as standard

7. Creating a long and heavy to-do-list

A long and heavy to-do list not only creates an impression of too much to achieve, fatigues the mind but also creates a cycle of unaccomplished tasks, which wears down your willpower.

Being busy is not necessarily being productive. You have to cut down on tasks to a manageable level. You have to assign or decline the one that you are not able to do.

Characteristics:

- Having a list of tasks that cannot be reasonably completed within a set time limit e.g. within a day.
- Always never finishing up on tasks on the To-do list
- Feeling overwhelmed and fatigued

How to avoid long list:

- Prioritize your items by striking a balance between the most important and the most urgent, giving importance to a one that meets the two.
- Limit your items to a maximum of five items.

8. Failure to automate recurrent tasks

With advanced technology, many tasks can be automated. You can automate tasks such as:

- Making coffee
- Boiling rice
- Posting on blogs and social media
- Supervising
- Washing clothes and dishes
- Etc

Solution

Record all recurrent tasks, map them out, program them and find ways in which you can automate them.

9. Failure to say 'NO' when you have enough

There are those employees who never say 'NO' even if they have enough work. Most of the time, this is driven by three factors:

- Trying to please your boss
- Fearing negative repercussions
- Lack of assertiveness

Solution

Learn to be assertive. Overcome your own insecurities. Trying to please your boss or fearing negative repercussion are both due to personal insecurity. Find the source of that insecurity and address it.

10. Waiting for optimal work conditions

There are many times when we fail to do certain tasks simply because 'the conditions are not ripe'. This is procrastination.

Solution

Everyone suffers from inertia at one point or another. The best way to deal with inertia is to do exactly that which you ought to do but do not feel like doing.

11. Hoping from meeting to meeting without clear-cut agenda and schedule

This is a problem with many managers. Some of them, as a company policy, are expected to have scheduled meetings. However, they fail to plan for the meetings such that they call for the meeting without a well-crafted agenda. Some meetings that would not have been necessary end up being created because matters that would have been addressed in the previous meetings were never addressed.

Solution

- Brainstorm with colleagues and do research before preparing an agenda
- Have a well-defined agenda
- Schedule sufficient time to each agenda item so that all matters are addressed
- Do not have too many agenda items as this will naturally force another meeting since not all of them will have been covered

Other bad working habits:

- Isolating Yourself – Most workplaces require team players for work to flow smoothly. Isolating yourself from others obstructs this smooth flow of work thus impairing productivity at workplace.

- Avoiding Work – Avoiding work not only denies your employer the much-needed labor but also denies you the opportunity to optimize your experience.

- Resisting Change – Change is inevitable and the only thing that enables an organization to survive perpetually. Resisting change may lead you to risk your long-term employability as neither your job nor your organization can survive in the long-term without change.

- Being Negative – Being negative results into a poor relationship between you and your colleagues or your supervisors/juniors. This may cause low work morale resulting in low productivity.

- Gossiping – Gossiping is a sign of inferiority complex. Gossiping is mostly fueled by jealousy. Gossiping may destroy work relationships thus resulting in enmity at work, which may cause negative conflicts.

- Procrastinating, then rushing – This is an erratic behavior characteristic of psychological instability. You work within a system. Thus, if you cannot go by the pace in the work system, you end up disrupting the normal flow of work thus resulting in the work system's overall sub-optimality.

Bad internet habits

The Internet is one of the most important information and communication resources of our modern times. Yet, there are certain bad habits that make us not effectively utilize the internet to enhance our productivity. Some of these bad habits include:

- Impulsive web browsing
- Checking email throughout the day
- Being tempted by internet apps and notifications

Solution

- Use internet only when your task demands it.
- Check emails during break times – mid-morning break, lunch-break and evening break.
- Some browsers have plugins that allow you to do online things that you would possibly do offline such as typing, use of spreadsheets, timers, clocks, etc. Avoid these temptations. Use your offline apps. Switch off the internet so that you do not receive notifications.

Bad social habits

1. Seeking attention by complaining – This is going to be considered as nagging and lack of appreciation. It may result in you being shunned or isolated.

2. Focusing on your inner monologue instead of dialogue in front of you – engaging in dialogue only comes from attentive listening. Focusing on your inner self-talk rather

than engaging with others may cause them to think that you are an aloof person.

3. Multi-tasking while you chat – This may make the person you are chatting with consider you disrespectful and disinterested in the chat.

4. Not paying attention to the people, you care about most – Social relationships need attention. Without giving due attention to people you care about most may lead to them feeling neglected and thus build resentment.

5. Constantly fishing for compliments – Wait for compliments to come on their own in the most natural way. Overtly seeking compliments may lower your integrity.

Solutions

1. Stop being a perpetual complainant

2. Listening to others instead of own self-talk while engaging them

3. Giving full attention to others while engaging them

4. Paying keen attention to loved ones

5. Avoid seeking compliments

Bad leisure habits

Leisure is extremely important to our productivity. It is the time to unwind from routine and recharge. However, abuse of leisure time can be counterproductive. The following are some of the bad leisure habits:

- Alcoholism
- Pornography
- Gossiping

Solution

Have a To-do list for your leisure activities. This will help you avoid deviating towards doing counterproductive things. Keep off a company that has a negative influence.

Bad sleeping habits

Poor bedroom habits can cause you loss of sleep, stress and even frustration. Poor bedroom habits have been known to cause strained relations between married couples. This could lead to divorce.

These bad habits include:

1. Having sleep distractions in your bedroom
2. Sleeping late

3. Waking up late

4. Putting your combs, mirrors, makeup tubes and other beauty paraphernalia on your bed;

5. Cluttering your bedroom

Solutions:

1. Remove all sleep distractions from your bedroom e.g. noise, powerful light, etc

2. Sleep early in the night, at least by 9 p.m. if you wake up by 5 p.m. This will grant you ample time to sleep

3. Wake up early from bed so as to avoid getting to work or school late, feeling tired during the day and reduce the risk of headaches and body aches

4. Spread your bed immediately after waking up

5. Don't clutter your bedroom by making it another kind of store

Bad health habits

These habits compromise one's health. Bad health habits include:

1. Poor hygiene habits

2. Poor diet habits

3. Poor activity habits

Poor hygiene habits

Poor hygiene is one of the primary causes of disease and poor health. The following are some of the poor hygiene habits:

1. Not brushing your teeth as expected

2. Not bathing every morning

3. Wearing clothes more than once a week

Poor diet habits

Eating is the only way you can refuel your body. You eat well, your body become energized and more productive. However, not all of us give priority to eating well. It is unfortunate that so many people care so much about what fuel goes to their car than what fuel goes to their body.

What would happen if a gas station attendant fills your car tank with the wrong or adulterated fuel? Most likely, you are going to sue. Yet, you do not take such a serious action when feeding your body on junk foods. Rationally, you should be more concerned about what goes into your body than what goes into your car.

Some of the common poor eating habits include:

- Bingeing – overindulgence in eating

- Substituting drinking water with beverages

- Avoiding cooking own meals (eating at fast food restaurants) – The problem with eating at fast food restaurants is that you have no control over the ingredients of the food that you are being served. Thus, you cannot be in a position to control your diet. It is almost inevitable that you will occasionally eat at a fast food restaurant. However, making it a habit is the problem.

- Eating junk foods – Junk foods are those foods that have very low nutritional value. Some of these junk foods include CRAP (Carbonated, Refined, Alcoholic/Additive, and Processed) food. These foods cost more than they actually give to your body.

- Eating bad sugar – Most people know sugar as the table sugar. However, scientifically, all carbohydrates are sugars. Bad sugars are those simple sugars that cause a sudden imbalance in blood sugar level, contribute to obesity and trigger diabetes. Extracted sugar e.g. sucrose (table sugar), fructose, and glucose, among others are examples of bad sugar.

- Skipping meals – It is common for people to say, "I am dieting" while it means that they are skipping meals. Skipping meals create a deficit in energy levels. This eventually lowers your productivity.

Poor activity habits

Sedentary life is characterized by lack of activity. Our body was made to be on the move most of the time. However, due to challenges of modernity, we find ourselves spending lots of time behind work or study desk.

Nonetheless, there are certain habits that we have accustomed ourselves to that makes this situation much worse. Such poor activity habits include:

- Spending most of your free time watching movies and playing video games

- Spending most of your free time on social media networks

- Not doing fitness workouts

- Not carrying out simple manual house chores such as lawn mowing, cleaning the house, washing dishes, etc

Good health habits

To be able to overcome bad health habits, we need to create have positive habits so that they can fill the void created by killing bad habits.

Good hygiene habits

1. Wash your face

2. Brush your teeth

3. Bath after workouts

Good diet habits

1. Stock foodstuff ingredients so that you do not fall into a victim of quick fixes in the form of toxic fast foods in restaurants.

2. Take breakfast everyday morning after a shower. Ensure that the breakfast has balanced diet.

3. Avoid eating when not hungry or under the influence of cravings

4. Avoid taking CRAP (Carbonated, Refined, Alcoholic and Processed) foods

5. Cook your own meals. Pack some for your lunch while at work or school. This way, you will not be tempted to go to a fast-food restaurant. You will also be less tempted to eat junk food or skip meals.

6. Take water after eating and when thirsty. Avoid substituting water with beverages, more so, soft drinks.

7. Practice clean eating, that is, eating food as close to natural as possible

8. Avoid bad sugars (added sugar and simple carbohydrates).

9. Take at least three meals a day.

10. Take meals in small portions, more frequently as opposed to large portions less frequently.

11. Have your diet schedule so that you can plan your meals. This way, you will avoid quick fixes.

Good activity habits

Your body needs mobility exercises to remain in good form. This is how it was designed to be. It was not designed to remain seated or standing for long hours.

The following are good activity habits:

1. Carrying out some workouts immediately after washing your face and brushing your teeth early in the morning after waking up

2. Taking short-breaks, at least after every hour, from seating while in office or study room to walk around, pick a file from the cabinet are converse with a colleague.

3. Stretching your limbs frequently while seated

4. Standing up straight frequently (at least after every 45 minutes, or so for a minute)

5. Having lunchtime light exercises such as taking a walk, doing press-ups, yoga, etc.

6. Having evening workouts after work or study.

7. Spending at least 3 hours of workouts over the weekend, possibly per day, if you are free on both days.

8. Carrying out household and homestead chores while free instead of hiring someone else to do cutting grass, mowing, pruning, sweeping compound, cleaning, washing, among others, helps to enhance your physical activity.

They are the best things you can easily do without even realizing that you are carrying out some form of workout.

Bad money habits

The following are some of the poor financial habits that you need to banish in your habit stack for finances:

1. Spending more than you earn

2. Not saving out of your earnings

3. Impulse buying

4. Making quick poorly-thought-out investment decisions

Solution

The following are good financial habits that you ought to engender as part of your habit stack for finances:

1. Spend within your means

2. Save at least one-third of your earnings

3. Plan your purchases

4. Take time to make investment decisions

Tools to enable you to manage your finance habits

The good thing about finance is that it has plenty of tools that can enable you to manage your finance habits.

The following are some of these important tools:

1. Financial Plan

2. Budget

3. Charts

Bad leadership habits

- Finding problems in everything – Being critical is important. However, as a leader, it should be measured and prudent. Otherwise, those who follow you may feel unwanted and thus give up.

- Never providing a positive praise – Lack of positive praise may be interpreted by many as a subtle sign of dissatisfaction or lack of recognition for others' efforts. This may lead to resentment.

- Struggling to make decisions – There is nothing that is as bad in leadership as being indecisive. Struggling to make decisions is a sign of indecisiveness. This may send signals that you are a weak leader and thus prompt your replacement.

- Failing to pay attention to the works of the people who are working for you – Paying attention to what others are doing on your behalf is a good sign of being caring and appreciative. Failure to provide attention to what is being done for you may lead to low morale of those doing it.

- Changing direction without informing other people that you have changed direction – Leadership is about forthrightness. People follow your direction. When you change direction without notice, this breeds distrust amongst your followers as they may consider you treacherous.

Other bad habits

- Keeping distractions – Distractions during morning routine, during work routine, and during evening routine will lower your productivity. Avoid noise, video games, etc during such routines.

- Not being decisive – Not being decisive can occur occasionally, especially when confronted with difficult choices. However, when this becomes persistent, then it becomes a bad habit. Most of the time, indecisiveness arises out of fear of repercussions. Take responsibility and be accountable. For so long as you decide in good faith and prudently, there is nothing to fear about its repercussion since a decision has to be made

- Not setting disciplinary measures – It is common to discipline others for their mistakes yet not discipline ourselves. Every time we fail to set disciplinary measures, we set a bad habit – a habit of not being accountable to ourselves. Without disciplinary measures, laziness and lethargy sets in. Our productivity becomes compromised in the end.

- Moral licensing – Moral licensing is about finding justification for our bad habits. For example, taking junk food simply because you saw your celeb doing it or sitting on a work desk simply because you saw your president doing it. There are many bad habits that we have moralized simply because they have become some sort of a 'norm'. A bad habit is a bad habit, whether normalized or not.

- Failing to plan and set goals - All that we have discussed above as bad habits are in one way or another relate to failure to set goals. Setting a goal is wide in itself. Thus, let us discuss it wholly in the next section.

How to kill bad habits

Just as you are capable of creating bad habits, you too are capable of killing your bad habits. The following are ways by which you can kill your bad habits:

1. Strengthen your willpower

2. Boost your self-awareness

3. Gather emotional support

4. Engage in sublimation

5. Practice substitution

6. Plan and set goals

- **Strengthen your willpower**

Willpower is the inner strength that drives you to achieve your intended desire.

- **Boost your self-awareness**

Self-Awareness refers to conscious knowledge of one's own character, feelings, motives, and desires. To be self-aware is to learn and discover who you are. By discovering who you are, you are able to establish your sense of purpose and use your willpower to pursue it to the highest possible end.

- **Gather emotional support**

Bad habits die hard. The easiest way to fight bad habits is to gather emotional support from your trusted family members and friends. They will offer you advice, understand your plight and encourage you to overcome them. They could even go further to offer you a reward for your success. This also makes it hard for you to revert to your bad behavior since you will not just want to fail yourself but also you will not want to fail your loved ones.

- **Engage in sublimation**

Sublimation involves replacing a primitive urge with a more creative one. For example, if you feel sexual desire, you may replace your sexual desire with playing piano or playing tennis. Thus, you haven't really satisfied your primitive urge for sex, but you have suppressed it by replacing it with a more creative urge for piano. Thus, sublimation is about replacing one urge with another urge but not providing an alternative means to satisfying the urge.

- **Practice substitution**

Substitution is about finding a better alternative that satisfies the same urge. For example, if you are an alcoholic, you may overcome addiction to alcohol by participating in tea parties rather than alcohol parties. This will serve your urge to 'drink and socialize' but by substituting alcohol for tea. Thus, in substitution, you don't suppress the urge, but find a better means of satisfying it.

- **Plan and Set goals**

Setting goals is extremely important in overcoming bad habits. Without a goal, you will not be able to achieve your target.

Without a target to achieve, there will be no commitment. Without commitment, there will be no discipline.

Setting goals is an important part of planning. In planning, you can optimize your effort towards achieving your ultimate goal – productivity.

In the next section, we will have a deeper insight into planning and setting your goals.

SET YOUR GOALS

Without a goal, you bump into life like a headless chicken. It is a goal that sets the direction of all your endeavors. There can be no productivity without a goal.

So, what is a goal?

A goal is simply an outcome (end-result) that you desire to achieve once you accomplish your mission.

How does a goal come about?

A goal does not arise from nowhere or out of nothing. **A goal is a product of a planning mindset**. Thus, without a planning mindset, there can be no goal. A goal is part of a plan. You cannot set a goal without a plan. Yet, you cannot have a plan without having a planning mindset. It all begins in the mind. In essence, productivity is an outcome of a planning mindset.

Create a planning mindset

Your mindset is the garden where your ideas grow and mature as planned. How healthy your ideas become depends solely on how you tend to this garden. Make it fertile and your ideas will become healthy and prosperous.

What is mindset?

A mindset is a set of beliefs, assumptions, and thoughts that make up one's mental attitude, habit, inclination or disposition, which predetermines a person's perceptions and responses to situations, circumstances, and events.

Why is mindset so important?

Mindset is important because it is the point of reference to which you perceive and respond to events, circumstances, and situation. How you perceive things depends on your mindset. That is why many experts say that 'you see things as you are' and not necessarily, as they are. This 'you are' is your mindset.

Mindset is the fertile ground upon which the seed of vision grows. How healthy and great your vision becomes solely depend on your mindset. A defective mindset will definitely yield a defective vision. A fixed mindset will yield a fixed vision. Thus, a transformational (growth) mindset will yield a transformational vision.

Why a planning mindset is a growth mindset

Plans are never fixed. The best plan is that plan that is flexible enough to grow with changing circumstances, situations, and events. A fixed plan will most likely fail since all plans are about unpredictable future. This future may not necessarily unravel as one predicted.

Thus, a planning mindset has to be a growth mindset if these plans are made with success in mind.

Vision: the place where your goal post ought to reside

Vision is the big picture of how things ought to be. Vision is what you would like to see once you have accomplished your mission and achieved your goal.

Why have a Vision?

The following are the key purposes of a Vision:

- It inspires you to take appropriate action

- It helps you to communicate effectively with an inner compulsion

- It helps you to marshal resources and rally people towards a common purpose

- It empowers everyone who is inspired by it to achieve it.

The three essential qualities of your vision

A. Core Ideology

A core ideology is that set of ideals that inspire you to marshal your mind, heart, and sinew towards achieving a certain goal.

There are two key elements:

1. **Core values** – These are the overriding principles that guide your life.

2. **Core purpose** – This is the key reason why you think you live.

B. Envisioned future

This is the picture of what you perceive to be your future.

C. Your attitude

This is your mental predisposition.

How to create a vision

1. Establish your core ideology

2. Break it down into distinct core values. Values are those essential qualities/principles that you believe are important in the way you live and work.

3. Blend your mission and core values to come up with an inspiring core purpose.

How to write down a Vision Statement

The following are key steps to writing down a Vision Statement:

1. Set the time frame

2. Write the first draft

3. Seek feedback on your draft

4. Rewrite your draft based on the feedback obtained

5. Share your vision

Mission: the key reason why you want to achieve your goals

A mission is the 'raison detre' or reason for your endeavor. The sole purpose of a mission is to achieve a given set of goals.

Key qualities of a good Mission Statement

A good mission statement should:

1. Describe who you are

2. Describe what your organization seeks to do and why it seeks to do it

3. Be clear and concise

4. Be outcome-oriented

5. Be considerate of your key stakeholders – Your family, your partner(s), friends, your colleagues, your employer, etc.

Salient questions that you must answer in your Mission

1. Who am I?

2. Why did I come about?

3. What do I intend to do?

4. For whom do I intend do it?

5. Why do I intend to do things the way I propose?

6. What distinguishes me from the rest?

7. How do I want others to perceive me?

How to develop your Mission Statement

1. Develop a compelling call

2. Clarify your goal

3. Capture and inspire your imagination

4. Manifest your core competencies

5. Motivate and inspire your commitment

6. Be realistic

7. Be specific, short, sharp and memorable

How to write down a Mission Statement

The steps for writing a Mission Statement are the same as those for writing a Vision Statement.

Setting SMARTEST goals

Without a goal, there is no achievement. It is like a body running without a head – such movement will be random, aimless and short-lived. A goal is an end that you pursue. It is a specific accomplishment that you desire at the end of your endeavor; the ultimate prize that you want to get out of your endeavor.

Why have goals?

Many benefits accrue to your endeavor if it has a goal. A goal enables you to:

1. Have a direction
2. Be focused
3. Plan on what you can do to achieve your ultimate end

4. Be disciplined
5. Be able to measure your success

How do you create the SMARTEST goal?

A goal that will enable you to be able to achieve the best of your endeavor is a one, which is the SMARTEST of all goals.

For example:

> *Enforce strict home and work routine within one month to organize my life, harness the power within me, optimize my productivity and enjoy a balanced stress-free life.*

A SMARTEST goal must be:

Specific: A SMART goal must not be ambiguous but specific. A specific goal is that which answers the questions of what (productivity); Why (so that I **organize** my life, harness the power within me, optimize my productivity and enjoy a balanced stress-free life.); When (within one month); who (myself); Where (home and work) and How (by enforcing strict home and work routine).

Measurable: A SMART goal must be measurable. You must be able to quantify your achievements. In this case, the achievement is strict enforcement of home and work routine within one month.

Achievable: A SMART goal must be attainable (achievable). You cannot expect to kill your identified bad habits if you have no willpower. You must work to strengthen your willpower.

Realistic: A SMART goal must be realistic. It must be such that you have both the ability and the will to achieve it. If either will or ability lacks, then, your goal is not realistic. Your will is expressed on how much you are ready to sacrifice to attain your goal. Your ability is what assets (methods, techniques, and skills) you have that you can use to execute your will.

Timely: A SMART goal must have a timeframe for its accomplishment. In our example, the timeframe is 'within one month'. A goal that is not timely is not a SMART goal for its chances of being achieved cannot be defined.

Empowering: You are not a robot. You are driven not by electricity or fuel but by your inner desire to perform. The greatest drive that boosts your performance is motivation. A motivated person is an inspired person. An inspired person is an empowered person. A goal should be capable of empowering you to strive towards its achievement. To be self-empowered is to ignite the inner inspiration that motivates you to be on a self-drive towards attainment of your set goals and objectives. To achieve this, first, you must have a transforming vision – a vision which you can easily peep through and see greatness. It must be capable of radically boosting your welfare. In our case, ***enjoying a balanced stress-free life*** is motivating enough for you to desire to pursue them.

Sensual: A goal must be capable of being felt. It must touch and impact your heart as you think of it. You must be moved by it. You must hold it sentimentally. It must draw the best of your emotional energy. In our case, ENJOY is such a powerful sensual feeling in our goal. It manifests that feeling of ***stress-free life.***

Transformational: A transformational goal is that which radically changes your status of things. One of the greatest causes of your lack of personal development is stagnation accompanied by eventual decay. Stagnation is costly, sometimes much costlier than motion. When there is lack newness and freshness in the way you do things, boredom and monotony sets in. Your rate of default in performance goes high. Your rate of accident also rises due to your state of low levels of alertness. A transformational goal will push you from that stagnant pond of status quo into a new stream of dynamism. In our case, **increased productivity and stress-free life** are extremely transformational.

Work on your habits

We have identified bad habits and provided appropriate solutions. The next logical thing to do is to work on your habits as part of achieving your goal.

Decompose goals into functional domains

Each goal must be implementable. To be implementable a goal must be broken down (decomposed) into simpler elements such as objectives and targets. Once broken down, the broken down or decomposed elements must be mapped to implementation units (functional domains).

What is goal decomposition?

As indicated in the introduction above, goal decomposition is the breakdown of a goal into simpler implementable elements.

Key elements of a decomposed goal:

1. The Strategy

2. Strategic objectives

3. Tactics

4. Milestones/targets

The Strategy

The strategy is the action plan intended to implement the mission to achieve the desired goals.

The strategy is further decomposed into strategic objectives, tactics, and milestones/targets.

Milestones/targets are achieved through effective implementation system.

Strategic objectives

Objectives are the various specific targets that you must accomplish in order to achieve a given goal.

How to create Strategic Objectives

For example, in this case, some of your objectives could be:

1. To create and implement morning ritual/routine

2. To create and implement evening ritual/routine

3. To incorporate physical mobility and breaks in my work routine

Tactics

A tactic is the short-term plan of action intended to be followed in achieving your objectives.

How to Create Tactic

For example, your short-term plan, in this case, could be:

1. Make a list of productive tasks and good habits that I ought to practice in the morning, prioritize them and organize them into morning routine/ritual.

2. Make a list of productive tasks and good habits that I ought to practice in the evening, prioritize them and organize them into evening routine/ritual

3. List possible physical mobility exercises and types of small breaks that can be done during the working day and incorporate them into my work routine.

This is a very simple example. However, an excellent tactic must lay out the second best (and even third best) alternative should the best alternative fail. The more the alternatives the more likely that your strategy is going to succeed.

Milestones/Targets

A milestone/target is an achievement that you make at certain stage of the process.

The importance of setting milestones

Milestones help a transformational leader establish whether the project is on track or not and take appropriate action to remedy the situation if a milestone is not met.

How to create milestones

For example, in a one-kilometer fitness jogging, you could have four milestones each of 250 meters. When you finish the first 250 meters, the first milestone is accomplished. When you finish the next 250 meters, that is the second milestone accomplished, etc.

Setting manageable targets

For a goal to be implementable, the tasks must be manageable - that is, the resources allocated to them must be such as to enable achievement of set targets.

How to set up manageable tasks

1. Break down your tasks into simple chunks

2. Allocate these chunks to strategic objectives

3. Measure and define each chunk in terms of

    a) Skills required to execute them

    b) Tools required to execute them

    c) Resources required to execute them

d) Time required to execute them

4. Rank each chunk in order of priority

5. Determine the overall time required to complete all the chunks

6. Use project management tools such as Gantt Charts, Network Paths, etc to allocate each of these chunks within the project duration

Implementing your plan of action

To implement is to carry out your strategy (plan of action) to its successful conclusion.

Qualities of an effective implementation system

Building effective implementation system with inbuilt enduring qualities:

1. **Agility** – This is the ability to adjust with speed and dynamism to changing situations.

2. **Adaptability** – This is the ability to change in such a manner to be congruent to the changing circumstances

3. **Persistence** – This is the ability to endure for long so as to achieve stated objectives

How to build an effective implantation system

1. **Break down tasks into manageable chunks** – Tasks should be broken down into smaller manageable chunks. Huge pieces of tasks can bring fatigue, de-motivation, and resentment.

2. **Seek the right skills required to execute each chunk** – Once tasks are broken down into manageable chunks, the next logical thing is to find skills suitable to execute them.

3. **Allocate the right tools to each chunk** – The right skills need the right tools to handle the required tasks.

4. **Allocate sufficient resources to each chunk** – Financial, managerial and other resources must be sufficient to match with task, the skills, and tools.

5. **Allocate timelines to each chunk** – Once each task has been allocated the right skills, tools and resources the next step is to determine the timeline for execution. Project management tools such as Gantt charts, Network paths, among others become handy in this endeavor.

How to carry out (execute) the implementation

An execution should be specific to each action. The following is an example of an execution:

1. Start off and fully implement morning routine by the end of the first week.

2. Start off and fully implement evening routine by the end of the second week.

3. Enhance work routine to incorporate physical mobility exercises and short breaks.

DAY-BY-DAY PLAN TO INCREASE PRODUCTIVITY

In the previous section, we have seen how a planning mindset is extremely important to setting your goals. We have also seen the importance of decomposing a goal into functional domains.

In this section, we are furthering this by providing you a day-by-day plan to increase your productivity. Each person has a unique nature and unique circumstances. Thus, we cannot pretend to provide a one-plan-fits-all template. Nonetheless, it is better to provide sample templates than not. What we have provided in this section are sample plans, which you can easily customize to your own unique nature, needs and circumstances. However, flexibility should not mean indiscipline.

Benefits of day-by-day planning

Day-by-day planning:

- Boosts your productivity
- Enhances effective utilization of time
- Helps you to achieve work-life balance
- Propels your personal and career growth
- Helps you to be more focused on your key priorities
- Enables you to live a purpose-driven life

Questions to help you reflect on your day

The following questions will help you reflect on how to plan your day:

1. What is the most important task that I must accomplish today to make it successful?
2. What am I committed to making happen this day? What is my key goal for this day?
3. In addition to my most important task, what are the three other additional things that I want to be done this day?
4. What must I do today towards being healthier?
5. How can I make today better than other days?
6. How am I going to inspire my mind towards positive stimulation?
7. In what ways am I going to boost my wealth today?
8. How will I enjoy my day today?
9. Who will I spend my leisure time with today?
10. What kind of feelings do I want to experience today? What am I going to do to achieve them?

Questions to help you plan your day-to-day specifics

- What time am I going to wake up?

- What is the first thing I going to do once I wake up?
- What morning ritual do I have to make me feel powerful, focused, in control and happy? What kind of activities do I have in this ritual to make me achieve this?
- What, when, where and with whom am I going to have breakfast?
- What tasks will I do in the morning as part of my morning ritual? At what time? In which order? Where do I do them?
- Which mid-morning snack should I take?
- What other tasks should I accomplish before lunchtime?
- What am I going to have for lunch? With whom? Where?
- What is my next thing to do immediately after lunch?
- What afternoon tasks am I going to perform? Where? In what order and at what time?
- What afternoon snack am I going to have?
- Are there other things I need to do in the afternoon, either between or after my afternoon tasks?
- How will I conclude my workday? At what time? (e.g. organize workspace, have end-of-day meeting, disconnect, etc)
- How am I going to spend my evening?
- What am I going to have for dinner? At what time? With whom?

- What am I going to do after dinner? Will I do it alone or with someone else?
- What bedtime routine am I going to have in order to end it happily, be ready for a successful next day and have a restful sleep at night?
- What time will be going to bed?
- What is the last thing should I be doing before sleeping?

Basic day-by-day plan rules

- Start day with a powerful breakfast encompassing high-protein meal with complex carbohydrates for sustainable long-term energy production.
- Activate your nerves by engaging in some physical activity to wake up your body. Stretches, walks, and sprints are good.
- Start with a task that meets your long-term objectives – it should be the most important, not necessarily the most urgent.
- Engage in an activity that stimulates your mind – it could be watching a 15-minute inspiration video or reading an inspiring article. A good piece of poetry can do.

Structured productivity

Structured productivity is about being deliberately purposeful in your productivity. This includes planning and scheduling your productive endeavors.

Components of structured productivity

Several components make structured productivity. The following are some of them:

- Evening ritual – This is a ritual that is performed at the end of the day as you wind down towards sleep time. Activities engaged in this ritual are geared towards setting your attention, mind, and body towards rest. It also involves preparing for the next day.

- Morning ritual – This is a ritual performed to help you successfully kick-start your day. It starts with waking up and doing all other things that make you ready to go to your daily work/study activities.

- Exercise – Exercises are geared towards activating your mind and body to optimize it for performance.

- Meal times – This is time to refuel your body. It is like refilling your fuel tank for the next mileage. Just as it is important to be specific about the kind of fuel to your tank, it is also important to determine the right meal for your body.

- Learning time – Just as a meal replenishes your body learning replenishes your mind. It is the fuel of the mind. We have seen the importance of the mind. You can't ignore your mind if you want to continue boosting and enhancing your productivity.

- Sleep time – Just as it is important to take your vehicle to a garage on regular basis, whether it is faulty or not, it is also important to sleep. You have to tune yourself to sleep even if you do not feel like, for so long as time is up. Failure to do so will result in more damage to your body thus lowering your productivity. It is just the same way you potentially incur heavier repair costs when you fail to take your car for service when due.

- Free time (remaining time) – It is always good to have some time where you can deal with unplanned matters that arise in the course of the day.

Simple day-by-day plan sample

The following is a simple day-by-day plan sample that you can customize to your own suitability:

- 5:30 am – 6:15 am – Morning Ritual
- 6.15am - 7:45am - Learning
- 7:45am - 9:15am – Exercise
- 9:15 am – 9:30 am – Meal 1
- 9:30 am – 12:30 pm – Frog eating
- 12:30 pm – 1:30 pm – Meal 2 plus break (30min)
- 1:30pm – 6:30pm – Time Allocation 1
- 6:30 pm – 7:30 pm – Meal 3 plus break (30min)
- 7:30pm - 9pm – Time Allocation 2
- 9 pm - 10 pm – Evening Ritual
- 10 pm – Sleep

Time allocation is specifically for our major work/study/sports activity. It is what you mainly engage in during the day.

Without timing, this plan is based on the following framework which you can apply your own custom timing.

- Morning Ritual
- Learning
- Exercise
- Meal 1

- Frog eating
- Meal 2
- Time allocation 1
- Meal 3
- Time allocation 2
- Evening Ritual
- Sleep

Morning Ritual (routine)

A morning ritual is a collection of habits that help you set up a good start for the day. These habits are created through repetitive actions each morning.

Pre-planning

Everything requires advance planning. Thus, to plan for a morning ritual, you have to do it the night before.

The following are some of the things to do:

1. Fine-tune your mind for the next morning
   It all begins in the mind. Tune your mind to accept the notion that you are a morning person. Even if you have not been a morning person, get rid of the negative notion that

you cannot make it as a morning person. You can use positive affirmation, NLP, creative visualization, and meditation, among other ways to reinforce the idea of being a morning person.

2. Tidy your space to use in the morning

   Tidiness is the most serious indicator of discipline. It shows you are prepared to make it serious. Untidy morning environment will most likely dampen your spirit. It triggers a sense of exhaustion and unpreparedness for the morning routine. If you are struggling to stay awake in the morning in your early days, you are more likely to surrender and go back to bed.

   Make your morning space tidy the night before waking up. Some of the tidying activities would include:

   - Cleaning and setting up your meditation place (if it is part of your morning ritual)
   - Making sure that your kitchen is clean (no unclean dishes hanging out in the sink)
   - Arranging the dining table (for next day's breakfast)

3. Choose your attire for the next day

Before going to bed, it is important to have a clear mind of what you will wear in the morning for fitness workout and going to work. To achieve this:

- Choose the right attire for your next day's occasion

- Make sure that your attire is clean
- Make sure that your work attire is ironed (if it is a one to be ironed)
- Make sure that your attire is within reach

4. Set your goals for the next day

Make sure that you set goals for each day. Two to five goals are enough, depending on the weight of each. The best time to set goal for each day is before the day sets in, that is, the evening before. This is ideal because:

- It enables you to have ample time to reflect on your goal and plan.
- It enables your brain to internalize your goal while asleep
- It helps to de-clutter your morning from so many things to think about thus enabling you to have a more relaxed morning
- It enables you to have an extra chance in the morning to refine your goal should better ideas arise after waking up

5. Set up your alarm

Your natural wake-up cycle depends on the state of your body. If you sleep late or are more exhausted, you are likely going to miss your normal wake-up time. Thus, you will need an external trigger to keep time. An alarm is the best trigger. An alarm ensures that you have a uniform wake up time.

It is important to set your alarm to ring at the exact time you want to wake up. This helps to avoid procrastination (another bad habit). It also helps you to avoid chances of developing the habit of snoozing your alarm (another bad habit).

Ensure that you wake up at least 2 hours early to your departure time. If you leave your house by 8 am, make sure you wake up before 6 am. If you leave your house at 7 am, make sure that you wake up before 5 am. Two hours will be sufficient to carry most of your morning ritual activities before departure. Overall, your early morning routine should not take longer than 2 hours.

Waking up

Once the alarm rings, wake up. Do not snooze no matter the temptation. This will reinforce your positive habit and help avoid fuzzy feeling due to snoozing.

Once you wake up, start your morning routine. The following are some ingredients of an early morning routine:

- Hydration
- Washroom activity 1 (brushing teeth, washing face)
- Exercising

- Washroom activity 2 (bathing and preparing yourself for work)
- Eat healthy breakfast
- Getting ready for the day (packing, etc)
- Reviewing the day's goals

Sample morning ritual

6:00 Wake up

6:05 Wash your face and brush your teeth

6:10 Hydrate yourself by taking 2 glasses of water

6:20 Exercise for 20 minutes (jog or do press-ups)

6:40 Do a brain dump (take notes) and review your plan for the day

6:45 Take a cold shower

7:00 Perform positive affirmations

7:10 Meditate for 20 minutes

7:30 Eat breakfast

8:00 Learn for 30 minutes (read a book, inspiring article, etc)

8:30 Eat frog

Evening Ritual

Evening ritual, just as morning ritual, is extremely important for your productivity. If you do not rest enough in the evening, you are likely going to wake up tired.

The following are some of the important habits you should cultivate as part of your evening ritual:

- Reflect on your day and record your reflections in your ournal
- Review your calendar/diary/task manager for the next day
- Implement your stop boundary
- Keep off every work-related materials plus other personal stuff
- Set your alarm
- Switch off all bright sources of light including screens (phones, tablets, computers, etc)
- Clear off your social media activity and switch off your phone
- Relax your body stress and strain through calming activity – stretching, yoga, inversion, etc
- Relax your mind for sleep – read or listen to a short fictional piece

Practice positive affirmation (meditate, visualize, pray) and appreciate how your day has been so far

- Set comfortable sleeping environment – comfortably set bed, dark room, fair temperature, silence, among others

2. Set Your Boundary stop boundary

Stop boundary is a time from which you stop all work projects for the day plus all other non-sleep related activities (such as watching TV, working on computer/phone/tablet, playing video game, social media activity, among others). The stop boundary should be at least one hour before going to bed.

Sample evening routine

- 6:00 pm: Get home, change, do some outdoor work/exercises
- 7:00 pm: Prepare and eat dinner
- 8:00 pm: Clean and do housework, do packing for the next day (including lunch) and other activities with the family
- 9:00 pm – 9:30 pm – Have a family devotion
- 9:30 pm: Review day's work, review goals (long term and short term), plan tomorrow's schedule
- 10:00 pm: Write in journal

- 10:15 pm: Get ready for bed (brush teeth, put on pajama, take vitamins, etc)
- 10:30 pm: Watch or read a piece of fictional work
- 11:00 pm: Switch off lights

Exercises

You can have light exercises after work. Light outdoor workout such as jogging or walking in the park is ideal.

Meal times

Have meal with family or a loved one (if possible).

Sleep time

Always endeavor to sleep at the same time. Keep it routine, irrespective of whether it is weekday or weekend.

Learning time

Read non-fiction work in the morning and fiction work in the evening.

Allocating and sing your remaining time

The bulk of your day will probably be spent working or studying (if you are a student) or some other activities such as sports (if you are sportsperson). We cannot fix this into our full day-by-day schedule, as each is custom to your particular situation. You can always adjust your full day-by-day plan to factor this while not forgetting to include other important components.

Full day-by-day plan sample

A full-day-by-day plan encompasses the following three parts:

Part 1: Morning ritual

[Fix in your morning ritual]

Part 2: Work/Study routine

[Fix in your work/study routine]

Part 3: Evening ritual

[Fix in your evening ritual]

Work/Study routine

This will depend on your work/study schedule. While some schedules are flexible such that you have control over it (if you are self-employed or senior manager), others strictly tight such that you have no control over.

Whether your work routine is flexible or tight, it is important to consider the following:

- Do not skip your meals
- Engage in mobility exercises
- Have breaks to relax or refresh

Evaluating day-to-day plan

To evaluate is to weigh the outcome against targets/expectations as you carry out your implementation. It is the key part of managing success.

In our case, we implemented a day-to-day plan to increase productivity. Under evaluation, you will have to review the result of your implementation against set goals.

In managing success, you need to:

1. **Devise effective measurement standards** – Without measurement standards, it is impossible for you to be able to determine performance. There are various established standards for each task. Your experience can also be used to create a reasonable benchmark to which you can use to measure performance. The standard should be challenging but achievable.

2. **Develop effective feedback reporting system** – Once you have devised effective measurement standards, the next thing is to have an effective feedback reporting system. This system is akin to the quality control section

within the production department. Every performance needs to be measured against standard and the outcome reported immediately for quick action.

3. **Layout effective control mechanism** – A control mechanism is that mechanism that helps to regulate performance such that any negative deviation is rectified.

Rewarding success /Reprimanding failure

A reward is a positive gain you get in making any given undertaking. In this case, when you achieve your target, you need to have some gain. Psychologists have discovered that reward triggers that 'feel good' part of the brain, which brings motivation to do more. Thus, rewarding yourself for your achieved target goes a long way in re-enforcing your motivation.

After evaluating the implementation of the day-by-day plan, the next thing is to reward yourself. Since this is part of structured productivity, this reward mechanism must also be structured.

The reward process encompasses the following steps:

1. **Establish reward criteria** – A reward criterion is a standard of attainment, which you have set such that an achievement of that standard is rewarded. For example, if

the target per day were jogging 3 miles a day, reward criteria would be, for every 3 miles of jogging achieved, you get to reward yourself with a good treat at the dining table.

2. **Create the most impacting reward mechanism** – A reward mechanism should be such it furthers your endeavor. For example, it is your desire while jogging to be fit and healthy. If you choose to take soda and junk foods at the dining table, this works against your endeavor – to stay fit and healthy. Thus, the food at the dining table should be such to help you boost your health. Such food should be a balanced diet of natural whole meal.

3. **Endow the reward** – This is the actual giving of the reward. Having a great treat at the dining table is the actual endowment of this reward.

In case you have experienced your very own cases of indiscipline such that they prevented you from successfully implementing your strategy, then, you need to reprimand yourself. This reprimand could take the form of:

- **Denying yourself the undue indulgences** - For example, if your target was jogging and you ended up in a bar. The next logical thing is to deny yourself from drinking at the bar.

- **Sacrificing other activities that are not important so that you can allocate more time to implementing your strategy** - Definitely taking alcohol at the bar is not as important as jogging. You may need to sacrifice this alcoholism for the sake of your jogging endeavor.

- **Keeping off wrong company that deviates your attention from your goals -** If it is due to your friend's undue influence that you ended up in the bar despite your plan to avoid it, then, you would probably need to avoid your friend at such times you need to go jogging. That is if your friend is unwilling to go jogging with you.

- **Sacrificing resources from not-so-important ventures into implementing your strategy** - Spending money at the bar drinking simply means that you still have money that has not been allocated to priory areas. Commit that money to priority areas and you will not have much left to indulge it in alcohol.

CONCLUSION

Life rewards not those who are hardworking but those who are productive. It favors those who are result-oriented rather more than those who are activity-oriented.

I hope information provided in this book has enabled you to learn how to organize your life, harness the power within you, optimize your productivity and enjoy a balanced stress-free life. It is also my sincere hope that you have been inspired enough to recommend this guide to your friends and loved ones so that they too can also benefit from information provided herein.

Thank you for acquiring and reading this book.

Good luck!

www.ingramcontent.com/pod-product-compliance
Lightning Source LLC
Chambersburg PA
CBHW061049220326
41597CB00018BA/2721